Ciao, Bella!

A Book of Poetry Inspired By You

Ronnie Joseph

PRINT ISBN: 9798869094322
EPUB ISBN: 9798869094339

This book is a work of fiction. Names, characters, places and incidents are products of the author's imagination or are used ficticuously. Any resemblance to actual events or locales or persons, living or dead, is entirely coincidental.

DEDICATION

for KB
quello che è scappato

Ciao, Bella!

We've said "hi" a thousand times before
So why did this one feel so different?
Eye contact was held a little longer
I stopped looking at you and started seeing you
Suddenly I was able to speak in tongues I've never known before

Ciao, Bella! É bello conoscerti finalmente.

The Girl in Yellow

The girl in yellow, a sunflower standing tall
Rooted in cracks on a black field of concrete
A spot of beauty in an otherwise dull world
Hair dancing in the wind like petals floating to
song "She loves me, she loves me not"

The girl in yellow, a sunflower standing tall
With her sun kissed mind, body and soul
A spot of beauty in an otherwise dull world
They say a sunflower chases the sun
So, what am I, chasing her?

August 9th

You asked me to write you a poem on a random
Wednesday morning
Reading my words made you blush fifty shades of
red
"Nobody has ever done something like that for
me", you said
I knew right then that one poem wouldn't be
enough
Little did either of us know then that the love we'll
share will fill a book

A Short Story of Attraction

"You're doing things for me" you say pulling me
closer as my lips travel from your ear to your
collarbone

"Feels like I do things for you too" you say as your
hand brushes my leg before arriving at my base
ready to climb

"Is this, okay?" you whisper even though we both
know we've never wanted something so badly

The Poet and The Painter

The poet writes line after line scribbled on loose
leaf paper
Each line stronger than the last, building a
foundation
A house of cards, fragile yet fortified with emotion

The painter exchanging service for room and
board
A new tenant armed with spackle to fill the cracks
of my heart
A pop of color to turn this house into a home

With her, I am home

What if Penguins Lived in the Midwest

I am on a journey of self (re)discovery
The me that you see is not the me I want to be

Been feeling like I left a part of me in the Midwest
So I ask myself "Aren't you tired of always being
second best?"

> My friend Kyle tells me about his boney
> knees

Ohio

I wish I had driven out to Ohio
In the dead of winter when you asked
Instead, I let snow covered highways
And blurry windshields keep me away

Truth be told I was terrified
Not of the journey but of the destination
The one night stand you wanted
Would have ended with me having a nightstand

You deserved more than I had to offer
For once in my life, I did the right thing
Even though it still kills me
I needed to put you first

I wish I had driven out to Ohio
To have told you I'm sorry sooner

Space Travel in Inches

There is 15.13 billion inches of empty space
between the Earth and the Moon
There is approximately 1 inch of empty space
between each of my fingers
Even when I say I love you to the moon and back
It doesn't compare to the feeling of your fingers
fitting perfectly between mine

I give you an inch and you take my heart
Or however the saying goes

Stolen Traffic Light Kisses

Red lights are never
L o n g e n o u g h

To show you how much
I l o v e y o u

The Painter

I'm far from a blank canvas
A body covered in tattoos and scars
I look at me and see a throwaway
She sees me as an unfinished work of art

She sketched stars in my eyes
And the moon in my heart
Even in my darkest, she lights my way
She's the painter I've been waiting for

If You're a Bird, I'm A Bird

If you're a bird, I'm a bird
Wherever the wind may take you
I will be right there by your side
Soaring through the air, wings spread
Looking for that perfect perch
To land and call our home
Wherever the wind may take you
I will be right there by your side
Feeling like I am already home

When You Know You Know

I knew I would love you
The moment I laid eyes on you
I'm reminded every time
You smile in my direction

My New Favorite Word

It takes
Two letters
Two people
Two hearts
To spell
US

    My new favorite word

Rainstorm

I want to get stuck in a rainstorm with you
You, completely drenched from head to toe
Each drop of water exploring your body
Is it possible to be jealous of the rain?

Back in our home, protected by our love
I watch from the doorway as you undress
Slowly as to not get anything else wet
Peaking over your shoulder you whisper
"I'm still wet"

I want to get stuck in a rainstorm with you
As we listen to the rain dance against the windows
In sync with the rhythm of Kind of Blue
From the safety of a bed filled with our love

Bucket List

When I turned 30, I made a bucket list of all the
things I want to do before I die
Before I knew it, I turned 35 and not a single item
had been crossed off
Things like seeing the Northern Lights or dinner
atop the Eiffel Tower
Taking in the wonders and beauty the world has to
offer

Little did I know that I wouldn't need to travel
around the globe
When the most beautiful site my eyes could see
turned out to be you
The day I met you, my bucket list became
complete

Dreaming Of You

I had that dream again last night
The one where you became my wife
Surrounded by our friends and family
All eyes were on you dressed in white

I had that dream again last night
The one where JJ came into our life
His little fingers wrapped around your hand
All eyes were filled with love

I had that dream again last night
The one where I woke up next to you
And realized my dreams became reality
God Damn, I couldn't believe my eyes

BABE

Before you came along it felt like
A light had gone out within me but
Because you're here now it feels like
Everything will finally be alright

Don't Wait for Sleep

When I was a little boy, I was asked what I wanted
to be when I grew up
My answers were baseball player, astronaut or
dinosaur hunter depending on the day
As I grew older, I realized just how out of reach
those careers actually were
Boyhood visions turned to college courses
stressing about the rest of my life
Who did I want to be, where was I going and most
importantly what was I to become

The "what do you want to be's" turned into "what
are your big dreams"
One day that answer stopped being a job but
rather a feeling of love and happiness
That was the day that I met you and knew you
were the dream all along
Now that I am older, I would like to offer some
advice
Don't wait for sleep to start dreaming
You may just miss the one

Thank God I didn't

Ocean Waves

When my lips touch yours
The corners of my mouth curl into a smile
Larger than the Atlantic Ocean
Waves formed by your tongue crash into me
I can taste the salt on your lips
And the warmth in the air
The thing about the ocean is it's forever
The thing about my love for you is it also forever

Storm Chasers

Our tongues crash into one another like
Violent ocean waves in the heart of a storm
A hurricane of passion and emotion
Nothing in our path is safe

The emergency evacuation route is a suggestion
For we are storm chasers looking for the thrill of
our lives
Our tongues crash into one another
Deeper into the storm we adventure

A Haiku for You

My heart skipped a beat
The first time I saw your face
Love was in the air

My Person

The days have grown dark
And the nights darker
Lost without a compass or a map
North Star hidden behind the clouds
Caught in a storm well offshore
In a raggedy old rowboat with no oars
Praying for safety, for land, for light
And then I found you, my person, my life

Save A Horse... (A Western Love Story)

Looking for a place to lie in safety
Through word of her mouth and tongue
She told me about a place south of there

I traveled across her mountains and valleys
Admiring the route stopping along the way
Making sure to take her all in

Land not yet settled tumbleweeds in the wind
As the sun sets against a purple sky
I rode into town stopping for the night

Headed straight for the saloon, thirsty
The doors on kneecap hinges swung open
Welcoming this out-of-town stranger

"What will you be having, Sugar" she says
All I could respond was "I am the cowboy"

Dance With Me

In the middle of the street
Lit by dim streetlights and distant headlights
Baby we don't need the music to sway
We have our heartbeats leading the way

Take my hand
Can I have this dance?
Tonight, and every night after

You've Got Mail

I always believed in rom-com love
The silver screen happy endings
I learned the hard way that life doesn't imitate art
That was until I met you

I learned that I've never been kissed
Or that you can't buy me love
But I can keep a notebook
Filled with stories of love, actually

I've never been the leading man
Even in the based on a true story
Adaptation of my own life
But for once, I got the girl

Streetlight

The sliver of streetlight peeking through your
window
Illuminates the twinkle in your eye
Silently screaming how much you love me

Half in the dark, half as bright as the moon in the
sky
I wonder if you can see how much I love you as my
eyes scream back
Kiss me goodnight tonight and each night that
passes us by

Today And Tomorrow

When the morning turns into day
I thank God for all the hours of light
How many times can I tell you I love you?
Power hour every hour the words pouring out
There are not enough hours in the day
So, when the day turns into night
I thank God for today and tomorrow

Forever

Today I decided that I will no longer do life
without you by my side
Tomorrow we will wake up to be one heart, one
body and one mind
Forever looks good on you and I

The Space Between Us

I often wonder if car manufactures built the
shifter knob in the center console so that lonely
people have something to hold

As winter approaches, I wonder if my cars center
console shifter knob will start to get cold

Since you now sit in the passenger seat, my hand
does not stop at the center console but rather
continues to occupy the space between your
fingers

I often wonder if the comfort I feel in your hands
is the feeling engineers dreamt of when building
the shifter knob into the center console

You're The Light

God proclaimed, "let there be light!"
And then he created you knowing
No matter where on Earth you'll roam
You'll make the world just a little bit brighter

How Can I Not Listen

She speaks in tongues
She speaks with her hands
Her mouth full of words full of love
Full of me, full of my love
When she speaks, I listen

Warmth

I've never felt warmth
Until your eyes melted my heart
Until your skin on mine felt like home
Until your lips whispered "You're safe here" as
they grazed mine

I've never felt warmth
Until you

Jazz

It's a cold crisp December night in New York City
The smooth sounds of Chris Botti's trumpet
Echoing between the buildings of Greenwich
Village
You and I tucked in the corner of the dimly lit Blue
Note Jazz Café

Stealing kisses to fill the silence in between songs
My fingers walking through your hair mimicking
the bass line
Hearts beating to the rhythm of love
Nowhere else I'd rather be than lost in the music
with you

A Blank Canvas Waiting to Become a Masterpiece

It's seven in the morning and I wish she could see
what I see
There's strength in her cheek bones standing tall
ready to take on the day
Under eye bags asking to be packed and taken on
a romantic getaway
Ocean waves flowing across her mouth in the form
of chapped lips yearning to be surfed with a kiss
But most of all, I see forever deep in her beautiful
piercing eyes
The kind of forever you only read about in
fairytales
Whether it's seven in the morning or midday,
there's nowhere else I'd rather be than lost in her
Already a masterpiece

Constellations

When I look into your eyes
The universe is looking back at me
Constellations made of iris freckles
Floating through the spaces in between
Crashing into your pupil planets
Safely returning to Earth, to you, my home

New Year's Resolutions

My New Year's resolution is to tell you more how
much I love you
Last year's hurt was checked at the door on the
way into midnight
I don't ever want you to feel that way again

There is no new year, new me
Just a new year and more love for you

Our Song

Our hearts beating in rhythm
To a melody only we can sing
Accompanied by an orchestra of moans
That could turn even the purest choir boy
To sing the tune of a man

What's Mine Is Yours

I position my plate, so my fries are facing you
Knowing you'll reach over with that cute little grin
thinking you're stealing a bite

I make the bed with the covers slightly off
centered to your side
Knowing you'll get a little chillier than me when
the sun goes down

I leave my heart open with the key in your hand
Knowing that I've built a home that's waiting for
you when you're ready

Guide Me Home

I'd sail across the ocean
Headfirst into the storm
Knowing you're on the other side
Your love, my guiding star to port

Storm Clouds

42

There are dark storm clouds rolling in
Turning brown eyes to grey skies
The storm inside you starts to expose itself
I brave the storm hoping to bring you to safety

Pillow Talk

It's amazing how after all this time
Your pillow still smells like you
But no matter how much I hold it tight
It will never replace the real you

Hoodie Weather

Today I wore that hoodie that you borrowed from
me
The one you'd wear in public so they'd know you
belonged to me
Freshly washed but the scent of you just wouldn't
leave
Each whiff of you, a punch that brings me to my
knees
This may be the last I have of you
Well, this and my everlasting love for you

For The Hurt

45

I write heartbreak better than I do love
Maybe that is why I self-sabotage so much
I do it for the hurt, for the pen, for the likes and
such

My Future

My heart, a roadside motel, mostly vacant
Wallpaper peeling revealing cracks to its
foundation
Inhabited only by memories too faded to fully
remember
Ghosts of those passing by, never staying long
enough
Only for the night

Until you, a stranger, opened the door and stepped
inside
Ignoring the dust and cobwebs, looking me right
in the eyes
You stayed the night a guest, the morning sun
shined
Awoken as a resident, a lifetime lease has been
signed

My heart became a home with a fresh coat of paint
A place you have been searching for to keep you
safe
Unpack your bags, stay a while, lay your heart on
the bed
I promise to protect it, no longer a stranger, not a
friend
But my future, my love

I Am Finally Home

I have lived spread across God's green Earth
Sometimes for moments, for months or for years
No matter where I laid my head at night
The other side of the pillow always seemed colder

And then one day I arrived home
A white suburban house standing tall in a
perfectly manicured field
I didn't have a key, yet, but I knew I had to get in
With windows like eyes to the soul
And a door painted an inviting shade of red

I finally found my home
In you

That Smile

It had stopped raining
The first time I looked into your eyes

I no longer needed rain boots
As the puddles from my tears dried

You're the gold at the end of the rainbow
The sun shined on me for the first time

All because you turned back the clock
And healed my hurt with that smile

Love Is...

Heart shaped pancakes
Cuddle puddles on the couch
Sneaking kisses
Talking about the future
It is you and me

Nothing More Beautiful

I want to take you to the mountain tops
To see the stars up close and personal
There's nothing more beautiful

Standing on top of the world lit by the heavens
I couldn't take my eyes off of you
There's nothing more beautiful

Than you

Goodnight, Mars

On a beach blanket counting the stars
As they reflected off of your eyes
For the first time in a long time
I was right where I was supposed to be

The space between us closing with each breath
As Mars lit up the sky a deep red
Of all the places, of all the nights
I was right where I was supposed to be

Goodnight, Mars

Once In a Lifetime

The kiss that changed my life
On a Tuesday morning at a red light
A once in a lifetime experience
Every time my lips touch yours

I feel bad for those that never felt
A spark so rare it's only existed
Between you and I every time
My lips touch yours

The Come Down

Our sweat particles colliding like cars on a freeway
Our hearts beating to the rhythm of the same song
Catching our breath like children catching fireflies
Watching the fan blades spin seemingly faster as if
hoping for liftoff
Watching you slide one pant leg on at a time
No need for a crowded room when we've got me
and you
Cleaning up the after party, a party of two

Makeup

He only sees you with your makeup done
Manufactured beauty we men are conditioned to
notice
Hiding who you truly are behind layers of paint
A white suburban home staged for an open house

He only sees you with your makeup done
I see you first thing in the morning, after a long
hard day
But most importantly, I see you for you
The you that's perfect for me

Happiness Is...

55

A calm lake sleeping beneath the stars
Currents rippling in rhythm to your breath
Your hand in mine

Pictures Of You

Think about how many pictures you're in the
background of
People catching your beauty but never stopping to
notice
Never the leading lady, always the background
extra

Now think about how many pictures I have taken
of you
You're always front and center for the world to see
Never again will you feel unseen
Beautiful, I can't take my eyes off of you

Across A Room From Start To End

In a crowded room you're the only one I see
Building up the courage to walk to you

If only you could see yourself from across a room
You'd see why I fell in love with you in the first
place

I will love you silently until the day I die
From a distance even when you're fully moved on

Suicide In E Minor

I used to find the beauty in everything
Even in the dead of winter
Knowing life was just around the corner

The trumpets continued to play
The same melodies of the singing birds
The sound of life in E Minor around the corner

Now I find myself being jealous
Of all the things that stay dead
Even knowing life is just around the corner

I keep reminding myself that April showers bring
May flowers
But does a flower even fragrant if no one's around
to smell it?
Life isn't just around the corner

Abandoned On My Birthday: A Sequel

Fifth year in a row
I threw myself a party
Surprise! No one showed

The Last Kiss

You never know that your last kiss will be your
last kiss
Now that it has, you can only think about what
you could have done differently
Maybe if the kiss was a bit longer or passionate
the spark would still be ignited
The flame wouldn't be so quick to fade

Instead, you stay in bed on your birthday
brokenhearted
There's no reason to celebrate when there is no
one to celebrate with
The world ripped out from beneath you
No fault of anyone but your own
Hoping your flame would fade quicker

A very (un)happy birthday to me

Glass Heart

My heart made of glass
Yours and yours alone to hold
Shattered on the floor

Us Against the World

I've always pictured myself more of a lover than a
fighter
But for you, I will fight until death
Never giving up even when you've given up on me
It should be us against the world
But for me, you are the world

Sleeping With Depression

I never understood why people with depression
spent so much time sleeping
That was until you left me
See, when I'm awake I'm faced with the reality of
you not being with me
See, but when I'm asleep I can dream of all the
wonderful things we used to be

I used to feel like a king in my queen-sized bed
that we used to share
Getting lost in each other's eyes, conversations
and entangled in each other's hair
It's just not fucking fair
Now I feel like a prisoner trapped in a hole
gasping for air

I took my last breath the moment you said
goodbye
The future we dreamt of thrown out of the
window to die
God, I'm begging you, I'm looking to the sky
Strike me down for without her I'd rather die

I understand why people with depression spend so
much time sleeping

Who I Used to Be

I'm probably going to kill myself soon
Not in the literal final stages of death
Just kill every part of who I used to be
It's not like they were working for me anyways

No longer will I wear my heart on my sleeve
Or believe in love at first sight
No longer will I give my all to someone
Who doesn't see the value I bring

I'm probably going to kill myself soon
I don't like the person I've become without you

Waiting

Last night
I dreamt of all the ways
You came back to me

This morning
I wait by my phone
Praying it will ring

Is Jazz Dead?

We danced to jazz records in the living room
Forgetting about dinner, burning in the oven
The smoke alarm screaming as the house heated
up
Not sure what caused all the smoke, the pizza or
us

Now I've ripped the batteries from the alarm
The screaming fell silent as my lungs fill with
smoke
As I burn the house to the ground around me
Igniting the memories of you, of us
Until one of us chokes

Tired

I haven't slept through the night in years
That is until you started sleeping next to me
Comforted in your presence, feeling safe and
loved
That is until you left, and I started sleeping alone
again
I haven't slept in months, not even a wink
God damn I'm so tired

Alone

This apartment does not feel like a home
Since you picked up and ran
Leaving me to move into it alone

Love Was Ruined

Love was ruined before you even walked in
You opened the door to a party of one
Music on mute, deflated balloons and stale cake
Party favors in the form of antidepressants laid
out on the table
Yet you stepped inside, closed the door behind
you and asked to dance
I fumbled through the records struggling to find
the perfect song
You put your hand on my chest and said "our
bodies know the music"
Suddenly I was not so alone, felt like I had a
reason to live… a reason to love

We danced for months as the world around us
passed us by
Somewhere along the way the speakers started
dying
You could no longer hear the music no matter how
loud my heart beats for you
I tasted love every time I tasted you
I didn't need medication to fake a smile
I didn't need to pretend I was okay… I was

Love was ruined again when you walked out
I'm afraid this time for good

I Promise to Find You in Every Lifetime

I see the things you post
But the things you post don't make sense
The things you post are the things you say you
want
But the things you say you want are the things I
was already giving you
The things I was already giving you are the things
you don't want in this lifetime
But I promise to find you in every lifetime

Colorblind

71

The problem with being colorblind
Is not being able to see all the red flags

Funeral

I often think about my funeral
I know a lot of people will show up
Truth is, none of it will matter
Because you wouldn't be there

I don't want a funeral without you
So, I keep on living even though I don't want to
Ironic considering the thought of being with you
Would make me want to see this life through

Everyone I Love Leaves

Honestly it feels like
Everyone I love
At some point
Leaves and I'm left alone

After they leave the
Color vanishes from the
Hydrangeas and my
Eyes fade to black

Snakeskin

When snakes grow, their skin does not
When this happens, they shed their outer layer
I often wonder if snakes are ever unhappy with
who they've become

I often wonder if I'll ever be happy again

Autumn Lane In the Summer

Leaves are falling on Autumn Lane
Like red and orange embers floating away
There is more beauty in death than in life

Death came early on Autumn Lane
Summer should be the season of life and love
Everything falls apart without you here

Free Solo

A mountain range of emotions formed
When who I was collided with who I became
Tectonic plates and the hippocampus shift
Creating a disturbance so catastrophic

Adventures with PhDs attempt to conquer it
Using every tool from A to Zoloft
Leaving me to free solo myself to safety
One tiny oval carabiner at a time

Somehow, they keep me alive and moving
My mountain range now feels like a mole hill
A few more steps down the homestretch
Until my feet are safely on the ground

Unfinished

The me you see and the me that I want to be
A vein diagram centered by a lack of confidence
An 8th grade science fair volcano begging for lava
to flow
A plagiarized book report scribbled after judging
the book by its cover

The me you see and the me that I want to be
A project left unfinished

Navigating Without You

There's no stars in the sky tonight
No light to guide me home
I'll make this drive until the gas runs out
Zero notifications on my phone

Shattered

You broke me
Shattered glass pieces
Of what used to be my heart
Never will I love another
Like I love you again
A soulmate shouldn't
Take your soul away
I am a broken shell of myself

Reality

I watch my apartment complex parking lot from
my bedroom window
Cars come and go
Spots fill and empty
If I stare long enough my mind plays tricks on me

I swear I see your car across the way
Underneath the flickering streetlight
Clear as day
I blink myself back to reality

And you're still nowhere to be found

It Never Is

The glow of a faint light in a dark room
A notification crawls across my cell phone screen

I pray to God it's you
It's not
It never is

The One That Got Away

"Right person, wrong time" is such a bullshit line
How can that be when you were put on this Earth
to be mine
We used to spend late nights taking long drives
Stopping at roadside gas stations and shitty dives

The right person would never leave your side and
stay
You motivated me and gave me reason to live each
day
I believed you when you said April showers will
bring flowers in May
But how can that be when my right person will
forever be the one that got away

Feeling Sorry for You

I wish we had fought
At least that would make this make sense

No matter how I replay us in my head
The truth is I was just never good enough

You ruined me
But it's you who I feel sorry for

I gave you my all
You'll never get that kind of love from someone
else

Sunrise Over Johnson's Farm

Going through life a shell of myself
The things I loved no longer bringing joy
You were the beauty in an otherwise dull world
Not sure I'll see another sunrise over Johnson's
Farm again

Bury me in the soil beneath the sunflowers
This way at least you'd need me for something
I told you I'd do anything for you
I meant in life and in death

A Promise

Despite it all
I'll always be
Just a phone call away
I'll drop everything to answer
That's a promise

Mirror Mirror

There used to be life behind my eyes
The sparks faded on lifeless dreams
I don't recognize the person looking back at me
Mirror Mirror on the wall
Please show me I'll be okay

Silence

The last time I saw you
We danced in the living room
To a Chris Botti record on the turntable

Since you've left me
Dust has collected on the needle
The sound of silence fills the empty space

You took the music from my soul
A parting gift, a memory of me
I live in silence waiting for you

Ciao, Bella!

Sitting in the spot where I wrote you that first
poem
The same spot where the sound of your voice first
welcomed me home
Reflecting on the last ten months
And how loving you had been such a privilege
Because of you, for a while there, the grass was
greener

Now I'm left with a "for sale" sign on my heart
I have to believe God's not saying no, just not right
now
I know you leaving was out of fear
But Baby, I'm scared too

I'm scared I'll never find another like you
A heart so big to wrap its arms around me
Eyes so comforting that made even the darkest
days brighter
Lips that often spilled those three little words of
safety… I love you

I will spend my days hoping you come back to me
I promised I would never give up on you
But for now, I'll have to say

Ciao, Bella. Spero non per molto, amore mio

ABOUT THE AUTHOR

Ronnie Joseph was born and raised in New Jersey. After moving to Los Angeles, CA for college and Pittsburgh, PA for a career, he finds himself back in New Jersey with plenty of inspiration and experiences to write about. Ronnie is also co-founder and co-host of the country music podcast, Outside the Circle Podcast. Ronnie can be found on Instagram and Tik-Tok at @ronniejosephpoetry.

www.ingramcontent.com/pod-product-compliance
Lightning Source LLC
Chambersburg PA
CBHW020132180726

47992CB00021B/2611